AF480919

The US Geography Book Grade 6

Deserts, Lakes, Rivers and Mountain Ranges

Children's Geography & Culture Books

In this book, we're going to talk about the geography of the United States. So, let's get right to it!

The United States is a huge landmass. It is about 3.8 million square miles. The geography of the United States varies by region from the east coast to the west coast. In fact, the United States is so large that it is divided into five regions:

The Northeast

The Southeast

The Midwest

The Southwest

The West

North Dakota
Minnesota
South Dakota
Pierre
St Paul
Wisconsin
Madison
Michigan
DETROIT
Lansing
TORONTO
Montana
Wyoming
Cheyenne
Nebraska
Iowa
Des Moines
CHICAGO
Springfield
Indiana
Indianapolis
Ohio
Columbus
Charleston
Pennsylvania
Harrisburg
Denver
Lincoln
Jefferson City
Illinois
KY
Frankfort
WV
Va
Colorado
Kansas
Topeka
UNITED STATES
Missouri
Nashville
North
Santa Fe
Oklahoma
Arkansas
Tennessee
Columbia
New Mexico
Oklahoma City
Little Rock
Atlanta
Montgomery
Georgia
Dallas
Jackson
Mississippi
Alabama
Texas
Louisiana
Tallahassee
Austin
Baton Rouge
NEW ORLEANS
HOUSTON
Chihuahua

CANADA
Edmonton
Vancouver
Regina
Winnipeg
Seattle
Olympia
Washington
Salem
Oregon
Helena
Montana
Idaho
Boise
North Dakota
Bismarck
Minnesota
St. Paul
Wisconsin
Madison
South Dakota
Pierre
Wyoming
Cheyenne
Iowa
Des Moines
Chicago
Illinois
Sacramento
Carson City
Salt Lake City
Nebraska
Lincoln
San Francisco
Nevada
Denver
Topeka
Springfield
St. Louis
California
Colorado
Kansas
Jefferson City
Missouri
Las Vegas
Los Angeles
Arizona
Santa Fe
Oklahoma
Arkansas
Memphis
Phoenix
New Mexico
Oklahoma City
Little Rock
Mexicali
Mississippi
North
Pacific
Ocean
Dallas
Jackson
Texas
Louisiana
Hermosillo
Austin
Baton
Rouge
New O
Houston
Chihuahua
MEXICO
Gulf of M
Monterrey

These regions aren't defined in an official way, so if you compare maps, you might see differences as to which of the 50 states belongs in each region.

THE FOUR MAJOR UNITED STATES DESERTS

The U.S. has four major deserts. The Great Basin, the Mojave, and the Sonoran Deserts all stretch from north to south in that order and lie along the eastern border of California. The Chihuahuan Desert is located along the border between Mexico and the United States. Most of the Chihuahuan Desert lies in Mexico.

Great Basin desert during winter

Great Basin

THE GREAT BASIN DESERT

The largest of the deserts in the lower 48 states is called the Great Basin. Even though we always imagine deserts as having hot climates, the Great Basin has a cold climate due to its elevation. Some regions of the Great Basin are located at altitudes that are at least 3,000 feet or as high as 6,000. A great deal of the precipitation there is snow.

One of the reasons that this desert gets such a small amount of rain is because the Sierra Nevada mountain range forms a wall that shields the desert from the Pacific Ocean winds. It's an effective wall because very little rain falls in the Great Basin. The desert lies between the Sierra Nevada and the other large mountainous region in the west, the Rocky Mountains. Most of the Great Basin's landmass is in the state of Nevada. However, Oregon, California, Utah, and Idaho all contain portions of the desert as well.

Sierra Nevada Mountains

Bristlecone Pine Tree

Sagebrush, shadscale, and a type of pine called the bristlecone are some of the plants that are commonly seen in this desert. The bristlecone is one of the oldest plants that have been identified worldwide. Scientists believe that some of these pines have existed for more than 5,000 years.

THE CHIHUAHUAN DESERT

The Chihuahuan Desert covers parts of Texas, New Mexico, and Arizona as you travel from east to west. In addition to various grasses, there are quite a few interesting plants that are commonly found in this desert. They are:

Creosote bush, which always faces southeast

Agaves, which have broad spikes

Yuccas, which have white flowers

Pricky-pear cactuses, which are edible

CHIHUAHUAN DESERT
NATURE TRAIL

Big Bend National Park

The Rio Grande River winds its way through the Chihuahuan Desert on its path to the Gulf of Mexico. Over 800,000 acres of this region are protected within the boundaries of the Big Bend National Park in Texas.

THE MOJAVE DESERT

The Mojave Desert has a broad range of elevations. Its highest point is Telescope Peak, which is a height of 11,049 feet. Its lowest point is in Death Valley, which goes below sea level by 282 feet. Because of these huge variances in elevation, the temperatures are extreme. The high elevations get very cold at nighttime. Death Valley is the hottest location in the United States with a record high of 134 degrees Fahrenheit. Less than 2 inches of rain fall there annually.

Mojave Desert

Joshua Trees

The Joshua Tree is a common plant in the Mojave Desert and ground squirrels, rabbits, snakes, scorpions, pronghorns, and kangaroo rats can be found there.

THE SONORAN DESERT

Spanning the states of California and Arizona, the Sonoran Desert is also partially located in Mexico. The Colorado and Gila Rivers cut through the desert. The area is quite mountainous and contains massive valleys, which get intensely hot during the summer months. This desert is known for its interesting saguaro cactus, which can get to over 60 feet in height. Lots of different desert animals live there as well, such as bats, owls, snakes, and turtles.

Sonoran Desert

Lake Michigan

THE GREAT LAKES

The largest lakes in the lower 48 states are called the Great Lakes. They're located in the northern part of the Midwest region and they are straddled between the U.S. and Canada. The border of Canada goes through four of the lakes and only Lake Michigan lies solely in the United States.

When combined, these lakes are the largest group of freshwater lakes on Earth. They contain over 20% of the freshwater that's above ground. The five lakes are:

Lake Superior

Lake Michigan

Lake Huron

Lake Erie

Lake Ontario

The Great Salt Lake

THE GREAT SALT LAKE

The largest lake in the U.S. that is not part of the collection of Great Lakes is the Great Salt Lake, which is located in Utah. It's so salty that it has more concentration of salt than the oceans have. No fish can survive in the lake, but some algae and brine shrimp live there.

THE MISSOURI RIVER

The longest river in the United States, the Missouri River, winds its way beginning from the west section of Montana and joins the Mississippi River north of the city of St. Louis. On its way, it travels through the Dakotas and Iowa as well as the Midwest states of Nebraska, Kansas, and, of course, Missouri.

Missouri River

Lewis and Clark were the first American explorers to travel the entire 2,540-mile length of the river. They used the river to navigate as they traveled west to discover the land obtained for the United States in the Louisiana Purchase.

THE MISSISSIPPI RIVER

The mighty Mississippi River is an important river in the continental United States. It travels a distance of 2,340 miles. It begins in northern Minnesota and flows south until it empties in the Gulf of Mexico off the coast of Louisiana. With its companion river, the Missouri, it's the river system that's ranked the fourth largest worldwide.

Mississippi River

Mississippi River

At one time, the Mississippi was the western border of the United States. Once the Louisiana Territory was bought by Thomas Jefferson in 1803, the river marked the beginning of the western expansion. It has always been a critical waterway for the transportation of goods from the Midwest to the Gulf of Mexico and it still is today.

THE YUKON RIVER

The Yukon River travels 1,980 miles and is ranked third in terms of length of rivers in the United States. Its source is the Llewellyn Glacier located in Canada. It flows in a northern direction to Alaska, then, it travels across the state and empties into the Bering Sea.

Yukon River

Rio Grande River

THE RIO GRANDE

The Rio Grande begins in the state of Colorado and winds its way for 1,900 miles until it empties on the western side of the Gulf of Mexico. It travels through the state of New Mexico. It's also the border that lies between southern Texas and the country of Mexico.

THE APPALACHIAN MOUNTAINS

Covering a stretch of land that is 1,500 miles in length, the Appalachian Mountains begin in Maine to the north and end in Alabama to the south. Mount Mitchell, located in North Carolina, is the highest point at 6,684 feet. At the beginning, this mountain range "fenced off" the first American colonies, but the pioneers soon found ways through the mountains. They followed trails that were blazed by Daniel Boone and other explorers.

Appalachian Mountains

The Rocky Mountains

THE ROCKY MOUNTAINS

Of the mountain ranges located in North America, the Rocky Mountains are the longest and extend 3,000 miles from New Mexico through numerous states and well into the country of Canada. Mount Elbert is the highest peak of the Rockies. It's in the state of Colorado and it towers from sea level to a height of 14,440 feet.

THE SIERRA NEVADA MOUNTAINS

Formed along a fault in the crust of the Earth, the Sierra Nevada Mountains are located primarily in California and partially in Nevada. They stretch 400 miles in length and 70 miles in width.

Sierra Nevada Mountains

Mount Whitney

The highest peak is Mount Whitney, which is also the tallest point in the continental United States at 14,505 feet. Giant sequoia trees, which are the world's largest trees, can be found here. Yosemite National Park and the resort of Lake Tahoe are located in the Sierras as well.

SUMMARY

The United States has four major deserts that are located in the west and southwest. In the northern part of the Midwest, the five Great Lakes hold about one fifth of the world's surface freshwater. The Missouri and the Mississippi Rivers join to form a powerful waterway from west and north, to south. Together they form the fourth largest river system worldwide. The United States has three major mountain ranges.

Appalachian Mountains

The Appalachian Mountains are the major range of mountains that run parallel to the east coast. The Rocky Mountains stretch from northern Canada to the northern section of New Mexico. The Sierra Nevada range runs along the east coast of California. The geography of the United States is filled with natural beauty from the Atlantic Ocean to the Pacific Ocean.

Awesome! Now that you know more about the geography of the United States you may want to find out more information about the world's mountain ranges in the Baby Professor book The World's Greatest Mountain Ranges.

www.ingramcontent.com/pod-product-compliance
Lightning Source LLC
Chambersburg PA
CBHW081603120726
47973CB00045B/71